GREEN ABOUT MONEY

A Graduate's Guide to Personal Finance

Congrats Jose!

Jeff ↑ my husband

José –
I'm *so* proud of you! I hope you read this book and utilize its priciples to lead & guide you to further success!
Teresa

GREEN ABOUT MONEY
A Graduate's Guide to Personal Finance

This publication is designed to provide accurate and authoritative information in regard to the subject matter discussed. It is not the publisher or author's intent to render legal, accounting or other professional services. If you need such advice, including financial, please seek out the services of a trained professional in the specific industry needed.

Copyright 2017 Jeff Tarman
All Rights Reserved.

ISBN-13: 978-1544258409
ISBN-10: 1544258402

No part of this book may be reproduced in any form or by any electronic or mechanical means - except in the case of brief quotations embodied in articles or reviews - without written permission from its publisher.

www.greenaboutmoney.com

GREEN ABOUT MONEY

A Graduate's Guide to Personal Finance

JEFF TARMAN

Presented to:

_____

From:

_____

Contents

Introduction 7
1. Commencing 9
   Step One 10
   Goals 11
   Examples of Financial Goals 13
   It's All About You 13
   Net Worth 14
   Earning 17
2. Banking 18
   Opening A Bank Account 19
   Keep Your Friends Close, And Your Bank Closer 21
   Banks vs Credit Unions 21
   Electronic Banking 22
   Understanding Your Paycheck 23
3. Borrowing 27
   Credit Cards 28
   The 0% Argument 30
   The Good, The Bad And The Payday Loan 31
   Now What? 32
   5 Steps To Eliminate Debt 33
   Home Sweet Home 35
4. Budgeting 36
   Establishing A Budget 37
   I Love It When A Plan Comes Together 44
5. Spending 45
   Straight Cash 45
   What's In Your Pocket? 48
   Are You A Subscriber? 49
   How Would You Like That Prepared? 50

    Live Below Your Means 51
    Missed Opportunity 52
6. Saving **54**
    Step Two It 55
    Habit-Forming 55
    Where Else Do I Save? 57
7. Interesting **63**
    $0 to WHAT?! 65
    Inflation 67
8. Investing **70**
    Getting Started 71
    Stocks 72
    Bonds... 74
    Mutual Funds 75
    Annuities 75
    Risky Business 76
    Are You Diversified? 77
    Cold-Blooded 78
9. Developing...**80**
    Success... 80
    The Future You 81
    Maslow's Hierarchy of Needs 82
    The Financial Parallel... 83
    Giving 85
    Self-Worth 86
Conclusion **88**
Glossary **89**
Further Study **94**
Appendix A: Financial Goals **95**
Appendix B: Statement of Net Worth **96**
Appendix C: 5 Steps to Eliminate Debt **98**
Appendix D: Monthly Budget..**100**
About the Author **101**

Introduction

green (adjective): Untrained or deficient in knowledge; inexperienced: 'a green employee.'

'CONGRATULATIONS!' I bet you've heard that a lot lately. I have quite a bit more to offer you than just that in our time together, but you should remember that sense of accomplishment. You surpassed a milestone in your life. Give yourself credit for that achievement.

Before you begin reading this, I would like you to write down the name of the person who purchased this book for you. I would assume he or she has your best interests at heart. I have designated a presentation page just for that purpose. If you purchased this book for yourself, feel free to pat yourself on the back. When you are done, we have some work to do.

Money is powerful. It can solve problems, and create new ones. It can bring people together, and tear people apart. We all deal with money on a daily basis, yet so many of us do not understand it and grasp its power.

I saw the need to address the topic of youth and money when I began to examine the consumer debt problem in America. Having spent three years in debt collections for a major United States bank, I saw first-hand the problems that Americans were creating for themselves. I talked to people in their 20's and 30's with staggering amounts of credit card and student loan debt. Most of them had no idea how big of a hole they had dug for themselves.

After studying the problem, I came to realize that ignorance plays a large part in this matter. They are simply not taught about money. Our schools are not doing the job to educate students about basic finance. The evidence goes beyond consumer debt into unemployment, welfare, and bankruptcy rates. The focus of this book will be on the foundations of personal finance that build wealth and breed success.

America has a problem that needs to be addressed, and the conversation needs to start at a young age. It's time to talk about money.

1.
COMMENCING

"Money is only a tool. It will take you wherever you wish, but it will not replace you as the driver."

—Ayn Rand

My first memory of being inside a shopping mall was when I was about 4 years old. I remember walking around with my mom and being hypnotized by the flashy store windows and bright lights. I can still picture myself looking around, stimulus overloaded and eyes wide open. I was amazed by the scope of it all. It would be moments later when my eyes would reach their full potential. As I turned around, I came to the realization that I was standing all alone. I had lost my mom.

With now swollen eyes and a pounding chest, this great new world had begun crashing all around me. As I managed to whimper out the second chant of "MOM" to that audience of unfamiliar consumers, I suddenly felt a hand on my shoulder. "Can I help you?" the man asked. Willing to trust just about anyone at that moment, I reached out. We walked past what seemed to be a thousand faces and turned the corner to find my mom walking toward us, having known where I was the whole time.

Are you lost in a world of consumers? Have you been distracted by your amazement of all the flash? I understand. You just need a little direction so you can turn the corner and find your way. I will show you how to apply some basic financial concepts to your life that will start you moving in the right direction. You will be amazed at how this great new world will change your life.

Step One

"A journey of a thousand miles begins with a single step"

—*Lao Tzu*

As a graduate, you are beginning a journey; a journey that requires sustainability. Whether you live to be 45 or 105, your ability to sustain life will hinge on whether or not you have your basic needs in place. These needs consist mainly of food, clothing, and shelter. The lifeblood used to provide these necessities along your journey is money.

MONEY: *A medium of exchange that is circulated by a government or official organization usually consisting of paper bills and coins.*

Money doesn't care. It has no feelings and does not discriminate. There is no political party that money favors more. A dollar bill will spend the same no matter whose hand it is in. Whether you treat it fairly or abuse it profusely, money will continue to do its job. The basic functions of money are as follows:

- A unit of account (measures the value of something)
- A store of value (holds value over time)
- A medium of exchange (facilitates transactions, such as to buy or sell) [1]

---

[1] Functions of Money. (2017). Boundless. Retrieved from https://www.boundless.com/business/textbooks/boundless-business-textbook/the-functions-of-money-and-banking-21/money-as-a-tool-123/functions-of-money-568-3194/

An important distinction that should be made at the outset of this book is that money is just the middleman. If someone physically handed you $1 million in cash today, would your life change at all at that moment? No. All that would change is that you would be holding a big pile of cash.

The change would most likely happen after you decided how to use that money and then put that plan into action. That is what we will focus on throughout this book. You can have the best of intentions as to how to use your money, but if you never follow through on those intentions, what good are they?

As you progress through these chapters and start to understand the best ways to use money, you should be focussed on developing your own personal plan. Remember the saying: 'Those who fail to plan, plan to fail'? A great way to begin the planning process is to start setting some goals for yourself.

Goals

"Setting goals is the first step in turning the invisible into the visible."
—Tony Robbins

The act of setting goals for oneself is extremely powerful. I am continuously looking at my financial goals to gauge my progress. Having both short and long term goals in place allows you to make your dreams become reality. Through financial goal setting, I was able to pay off my home in just three years and eliminate my credit card debt.

I view goals as being a light to the path of life. If you don't have a way to see what's ahead, it's really hard to make your way forward. Designate a place to write down your own goals while you make your way through this book or use the form in this book (Appendix A).

You will find goals to be very attainable when you have them in front of you. By seeing them on paper, they become real. Break them down one by one and focus on each of them, individually. When you complete one, check it off your list and write another one. Eventually, you'll start checking them off like it's your job.

Continuous progress is essential in order to make headway on your goals. That means you need to gather momentum. Have you ever just started running down a hill? You think it's fun for the first few steps and then you feel yourself start to move faster and faster. Then when your legs just can't keep up anymore. They eventually succumb to the velocity and you just tumble the rest of the way. That is the kind of momentum I'm talking about. The get-out-of-my-way momentum.

To get that, you need to start small and start today. There's no time like the present. Your day-to-day choices are extremely relevant when dealing with money. You aren't going to make one giant decision about your finances and suddenly have everything figured out. You need to commit to planning your financial future every day. Remember that as we go through each chapter.

One final thought to remember with goal-setting is to be specific. Don't write down "Make $1 million". That is not specific. Instead, break down your goals between short and long term in duration. If your dream is to become a millionaire, give yourself a reasonable time frame to do that. Can you do it in 15, 18, 20 years? If so, break that up into smaller, more attainable goals. That makes the task so much less daunting.

As you lay out your long term goals, be thinking of what you need to do on a short-term basis to stay on track with those goals. For example, "Have my car loan paid off by the end of this year." Along with that: "Commit to saving 15% of my paycheck." Your short term goals are the lights that keep you going along your path.

Examples of Financial Goals

Long Term
"Have $1 million in savings by (enter date)."
"Have no debt, including home, in 10 years."

Mid Term
"Have $100,000 in savings by (enter date)."
"Have $XX,000 saved by this time next year."

Short Term
"Have $500 saved in cash in the next 2 weeks."
"Move up one pay grade by December."

However you decide to map out your future, be specific and be determined. There is nobody else that has a more vested interest in you ~ than you.

It's All About You

You are the driver in your journey through life, so be responsible for the route you take. As adults, we all have to shoulder the burden of our own wants and needs. Understand that being personally responsible for yourself throughout your life is important. It is fantastic to have a loving support group around you, but don't allow yourself to become a financial burden to anyone. This will only create a ceiling on how high you can go in life to become the person you want to be.

You are generally free to move in whichever direction you decide in life. Your ongoing assignment is to make sure you are on the right track. This means you need to continually evaluate your current financial position. This includes how much money you need, how much you owe, and how much money you want. You should be your toughest critic on this evaluation.

In order to move forward from here, you need to have a starting point. We all start somewhere, and those places are vastly different from person to person. This is your time to plant a flag in the ground and own your current financial situation. It's time to find your net worth.

Net Worth

I want you to take stock of your life. One way to do that is to find out where you stand financially in your current situation. This is done by calculating your net worth.

Net Worth: The financial result of subtracting an individual's liabilities from his or her assets.

You cannot hide from your net worth. It exists whether you decide to recognize it or not. If a man over 40 years old has a poor diet and even worse exercise routine, there's a good chance that he has high blood pressure. He is probably aware of that without having to go to the doctor to get a test. His blood pressure exists whether he wants to know the number or not. The same is true of your net worth.

Banks, investors, and other financial institutions use net worth to get a snapshot of a person's current financial situation. To find your net worth, refer to the net worth worksheet (Appendix B) and follow along. To start this process, we need to calculate the total value of your assets.

Assets (Things of Value)

Asset: Something of value owned by an individual or company.

Assign a monetary value to all of your assets. This value should be based on what you can get for them in the marketplace if you had to sell them in a relatively short period of time.

Here is a list of common assets:

- Real Estate
- Automobiles
- Jewelry
- Stocks, Bonds, Cash

We aren't going to dig too deep into this right now. For the purpose of this exercise, you can leave out most things under $40-50 that you could not sell relatively easily. We are going for an overall snapshot of what you own. Try this exercise in more detail after you finish this book.

Next, we need to examine your liabilities.

Liabilities (Things you Owe)

Liability: Something that is owed or that an individual or company is responsible for.

Understand that most people have some type of debt. If you are just coming out of school, you may have a fair amount of student loans. You may also have a car payment. Do you have any other payments that you make on a routine basis? Take a look at these common examples and then add up all your liabilities.

- Cell phone/Computer
- Loans (Student, Car, Personal, etc)
- Mortgage
- Credit Card Debt

Calculate Your Net Worth

Now it's time to calculate your net worth. This is done by taking the value of your assets and subtracting your liabilities. Once you have done that, enter that number at the bottom of the worksheet. This is your total net worth. And yes, this can be a negative number; especially if you are just out of college.

Don't get discouraged about your number. The reason we are going through this exercise is to make you aware of your current situation. If you are a student just out of college right now, you need to understand that you are not alone if you have a large amount of student loans. This has become a major issue in our country. But do not allow yourself to be a victim. Focus on applying what you've learned in the classroom to the real world and turn that knowledge into dollars.

Your job now is to start setting goals to improve your net worth by paying down any debt you have, along with building your savings. Your net worth should be on a continuous path upward. To make that happen we need to talk about your greatest asset; your ability to earn.

Earning

Earning money is vital to your survival. I don't believe it is the most important thing in life, but it is necessary in order to follow through on what actually is most important to you. No matter how you earn money, make sure it is sufficient to sustain you throughout your entire life.

Whether you make $30,000 a year or $230,000 a year, your ability to earn money is what will propel you forward in the wealth building process. That steady inflow of cash is what will create your fortune later in life, so long as you follow a well thought out plan (keep reading) and continue to attain your goals.

CONGRATULATIONS, You did it! You took the first step on your financial journey. Starting is the hardest part, and that is now done. Check that off your list. You now have momentum, so keep going. Step by step you will progress through one of the most important areas of your life; personal finance.

2.
BANKING

"A bank is a place that will lend you money if you can prove that you don't need it."

—*Bob Hope*

B-A-N-K. Yep, that's a four letter word. Banks have not made it very easy for consumers to appreciate or even patronize them in recent years. In some cases, they have made Americans (especially taxpayers) furious. Stay with me though, because we need them. We have a symbiotic relationship with banks. Yes, they profit off of us; but profit is not a four-letter word.

Financial institutions are an integral part of our economy. They take risks on us (sometimes too many), they connect us to our local merchants and give our money a place to grow and feel safe. Understanding how they operate is an important part of having a solid foundation in basic finance.

Perhaps the most important principle in the operation of a bank is interest.

Interest: The money paid by the borrower to the lender as a result of a loan or other financial obligation.

Banks make money on the interest they receive from the money they lend. Banks can borrow from other banks to get capital (money) or go directly to the Federal Reserve Bank.

Federal Reserve Bank: The central bank of the United States whose duties include commercial lending and the control of money.

The Federal Reserve Bank lends to banks at a discounted rate called, appropriately enough, the discount rate.

Discount Rate: The interest rate charged by the Federal Reserve Bank when lending to commercial or other member banks.

So when you walk into a bank and ask to get a car loan, the bank representative will naturally be very happy to see you since lending is how banks make money. But let's back up a little bit and talk about starting a relationship with a bank first.

Opening A Bank Account

Walking into a bank can make some people feel uncomfortable. However, if you do your homework ahead of time, this process should be relatively easy. The key is to know what kind of account you need before you walk in. Don't get sold.

A savings and checking account are the most you will need right away. In fact, if possible, just go with a checking account. Your main goal is to have an account with a debit card that you can use for daily expenses. Don't get caught up on the interest rates or let them sell you on something you don't need (like overdraft protection). Overdraft protection? Really? Don't spend more than you have. That's your overdraft protection.

Overdraft: *An account deficit resulting from processing a transaction for more money than an account holds.*

You don't want to be in a situation that causes an overdraft. Most banks charge a hefty fee when you spend money that you don't have (like $30-$40). If you don't make a lot of money, that penalty could really throw you off for the month. That's why we don't play that game. Make that decision in your mind right now. NO OVERDRAFTS!

When you're talking to a bank representative, it's alright to say 'no.' Unfortunately, retail banking is mostly just a sales machine. You may come across bank representatives that offer you things you don't need. But you already know what you need: basic checking. No frills. The bottom line is to look for an account that has little to no fees. You can always add other options later if you decide you want some extras.

Banks have now moved to more of a fee-based platform to generate revenue as a result of the low interest rates in the last decade. Newer financial regulations have also been a contributor to that shift as well. Make sure to find out what fees your bank charges ahead of time, so you're not surprised when you get your monthly statement.

Keep Your Friends Close, And Your Bank Closer

I check my bank account every morning when I wake up. I do this mainly for two reasons: To check for accuracy and to stay on track with my goals. Your money is your responsibility. Are you paying attention?

Banks assess fees to generate revenue in order to maintain their operating expenses. Banks have goals just like you and me, however, they refer to them as forecasts or projections. They strive to gain customers while also generating a profit for their shareholders. And when they don't meet those goals (they call it missing their expectations) the consequences are reflected in their stock price.

Some examples of the fees that banks charge are:

- Overdraft fees
- Wire Transfer fees
- Maintenance fees
- Minimum Balance fees
- ATM fees

Banks vs Credit Unions

Think you may want to try and avoid some of those fees? You may want to look into joining a credit union.

Credit Union: A non-profit financial organization operated under a member-owned structure.

Not all credit unions are the same, but you may find some benefits such as lower interest rates and lower fees. Because credit unions pass their earnings/profits along to their members, they can offer these perks. Another benefit is that you are part of a community. A credit union may participate in making their city a better place to live by investing in their local community.

A downside to credit unions is that not all people can join them. You have to qualify (to some degree) to be a part of a credit union. The majority of the time this consists of living in the same district or working at a particular place of employment. They also may not be able to compete with the big banks in terms of technology. So if you are looking for the latest mobile banking perks, make sure to find out what your local credit union offers before you sign on the dotted line.

Electronic Banking

Almost everyone has access to online banking these days. Overall, this is a step forward in how we handle money. The speed with which funds are now transferred has made our economy much more efficient. However, electronic banking can have its problems as well. Here's a secret:

BANKS CAN MAKE MISTAKES!

I have had to call my bank on multiple occasions to correct issues that were wrong with my account. I'll say it again: pay attention to the fees. And always check your statements and receipts for clerical errors. Banks are comprised of humans, and humans make mistakes. The benefit in having access to your account 24/7 is that you can see these things and correct them right away.

Perhaps the most important thing to remember in any type of banking is limiting access. When dealing with electronic access, make sure your information is secure. Never give your banking information to anyone unless it is absolutely necessary! That includes significant others as well. Unless you are married, keep your account to yourself.

Direct Deposit

Direct Deposit: An arrangement in which electronic funds, such as salaries, are deposited directly into a recipient's account.

So where does direct deposit fit in terms of limiting access? Well, considering that your employer has most of your personal information anyway, I would not have any reservations about using direct deposit. In some cases, you may even get your paycheck a day early if you use this feature.

Most mid to large-size employers outsource their payroll to professional services. Having direct deposit available to you is a benefit due to the speed with which these companies can streamline the payroll process. Payroll service companies have a vested interest in treating your information with care.

Understanding Your Paycheck

I remember my first paycheck. I was working at a home furnishings store in my hometown in Minnesota. My job was to handle the store inventory of refrigerators, stoves, washers/dryers, couches, chairs and anything else that weighed more than I did. In return for my labor, I received $5 per hour.

The employer was a local small business, and they handled all the payroll in-house. We had hand-written checks and pay stubs, which didn't really make any difference to me since my focus was mainly on the amount of the check. I was a little surprised when I got that first check. It just didn't seem like enough (it never is, right?).

When you get paid, do you take the time to go over your paycheck or do you just look at the bottom line? You should be familiar with some of the basic payroll terms that are used today and be able to keep track of where your money is going. Let's break down a few of those terms right now.

Much of the information on your paycheck is fairly straightforward and directed toward you. Total hours worked, your wage or hourly rate, and paid time off (PTO) can be deciphered fairly easily. One distinction that can be made regarding your pay is the difference between gross and net income. You will find both of these on your paycheck.

Gross Income: Total income before deductions such as taxes and insurance.

Net Income: The income that remains after deductions such as taxes and insurance.

In addition to knowing your take home pay, you will also need to be aware of the taxes you are subjected to. You will likely have both state and federal tax withheld from your paycheck.

Withholding: The portion of earned income that is held back or deducted for purposes such as taxes and insurance.

An example of taxes that are withheld from paychecks on the federal level is the money the government takes to allocate to Social Security and Medicare.

Social Security: A U.S. federal social program designed to give financial assistance to its citizens.
Medicare: A U.S. federal health program set up for the benefit of the citizens.

These two programs are deducted from paychecks by authority of a United States law called the Federal Insurance Contributions Act, or FICA.

Federal Insurance Contributions Act (FICA): A U.S. governmental law requiring the withholding of earned income, typically from a paycheck, to subsidize the funding of programs such as Social Security and Medicare.

You may also be required to pay income tax on the state level as well. This will depend on where you live. Your state income tax would be listed in the same section of your paycheck as your federal tax. The total of those numbers is then deducted from your gross income along with other items such as your health insurance, 401k deductions, and Health Savings Account (HSA) contributions.

Health Savings Account (HSA): A tax-advantaged savings account for medical purposes that is set up for individuals covered by high-deductible health plans.

Some additional information on your paycheck may include your tax status (such as 'Married' or 'Single') and withholding allowances (0, 1, 2, etc).

Withholding Allowance: *Exemptions made by employees on their tax forms to determine appropriate deduction amounts from their earned income.*

Understanding where the money from your paycheck gets distributed is another way to remove the stigma from the payroll process. Pay attention to the various places that your money is being directed to. This will keep you on top of your finances and allow you to continue to focus on attaining your financial goals.

Banks don't have to be adversaries in our quest for financial safety. If we understand how they operate, the fear factor associated with these institutions decreases exponentially. Whichever financial institution you choose, be sure you understand what fees they charge and how they operate. Do your homework and find a financial institution that you feel comfortable with to start handling your money.

3.
BORROWING

"Creditors have better memories than debtors."

—*Benjamin Franklin*

I'm sure you've heard the advice, seen the advertisements, and read the horror stories about credit card debt. I seem to hear a commercial about how to get out of credit card debt on a daily basis. Personally, I fell into that trap myself. That is a small part of the reason why I decided to write this book.

Borrowing money is dangerous; especially if you don't have a plan to repay it. Once I decided that I was not going to be held captive by my credit cards, my mindset immediately changed. I realized the meaningless consumer wants that I was chasing were leading me down a path of mediocrity. And I am not mediocre.

So if you're looking for ways to avoid falling into financial traps, I'd like to convey a very easy solution to you that could save you thousands of dollars and keep you ahead of your peers:

DON'T GO INTO DEBT IN THE FIRST PLACE!

I made some mistakes in my 20's with credit cards. I had my own business and always assumed that I would be able to pay off the debt 'later.' Time is a funny thing, though. It can get away from you. Trust me when I say: "It's later than you think."

Credit Cards

"No man's credit is as good as his money."

—*John Dewey*

Now before we go further, I feel it necessary to point out a common misconception: credit is not money. Credit cards are a debt instrument. Sure, they spend just like debit cards and cash, but they are much more dangerous.

Just like the student loans that many of you have (or will have), credit cards will have to be repaid with money at a future date. And when that future date comes, you will most likely be paying back a much higher amount.

As Americans, we are living in a gotta-have-it, buy-now-pay-later time in our history. Point your finger at the media if you want, but at the end of the day, advertisers won't pay your credit card bills. You create your own destiny. The earlier you understand the concept of personal responsibility, the better off you will be in life.

The fact is that our society has become numb to the swipe. Whether it's a credit or a debit card, consumers reach for that little savior in their pocket to pay for everything from a pack of gum to a new car. Paying with cash is becoming extremely difficult. You, as a consumer, need to fight the urge to have anything you want, whenever you want it. There is an old adage that says: "Cash is King." Write that down and stick it on the mirror in your bathroom as a daily reminder.

If you do swipe that card, however, do everything you can to pay off the balance within the 21 day grace period. Credit card companies normally give consumers 21 days to pay the charges without any interest being charged. Take advantage of that so you aren't hit with the high interest rates that many cards charge when you carry a balance with them.

Having worked in the collections industry for a major United States bank, I can tell you the damage that can be done by abusing credit cards can be disastrous. Credit cards are a privilege, not a right. If you abuse that privilege, you may not get another chance to be given the opportunity again. Or, at the very least, you will spend a very long time trying to build your credit back up to the point of being able to secure a card with a decent rate of interest.

But honestly, you shouldn't even need a credit card in the first place. They are just a gateway to more debt. Do not justify charging anything on a credit card. That is simply the debtor mentality. Those who have amassed fortunes are not in the position they are in as a result of having a credit card.

Perhaps we need a little history refresher course. Let's take a quick look back to the Great Depression. Do you think the banks were giving out credit back then? Of course not. Money was extremely tight at that time. They didn't have credit lines, they had bread lines. If you were lucky enough to have a job, you saved every cent of the money that you didn't need for basic living.

If you think something like the Great Depression can't happen again, you're not being honest with yourself. Just recently, the Great Recession caused millions of Americans to lose their jobs. I am here to tell you that it could have been a lot worse.

Why wasn't it? That is arguable, but we essentially kicked the can down the road for someone else to pick up. The U.S. issued the largest stimulus plan in history. You can think of it as a $787 billion charge on the country credit card. Don't attempt to solve a problem by spending your way out. Stay away from credit cards and debt in the first place.

The 0% Argument

I'm sure there are some of you reading this that think you have the system beat. Maybe you received a credit card in the mail that had a 0% interest rate attached to it and you decided to use that card for all your purchases. No interest! You won, right? The 0% argument is a slippery slope indeed.

It starts innocently enough. 'I'll just use it for gas' you say. Then, 'let's go out for a nice dinner we deserve it.' Suddenly you have an emergency. The car starts making a grinding noise that even you can tell is definitely not normal. You need new brakes. Now, you have a $1700 credit card balance. But it's alright because it's 0% financing. Plus it's nice only having to pay the minimum payment.

6 months down the road, and 6 months worth of thinking you deserve things you can't afford, you now have a credit card with a $3200 balance and nothing to show for it. You start to wonder how this happened in the first place. How is your life better now than it was when you didn't owe all this money?

The next day you come home from work and grab the mail on your way in. You flip through the junk and that's when you notice your credit card statement. You open it up to check the due date, knowing that you don't get paid until next week. That's when you see it: 27.59%. You look at the statement to make sure you didn't open someone else's mail; it's yours. Then you start to read. The party's over. The interest rate on the card was a teaser rate.

Teaser Rate: A low introductory rate of interest offered for a fixed period of time in an attempt to gain new clients.

The 0% argument is a fool's paradise. Instead of trying to see how close to the snake you can get before getting bit, just submit to the fact that it is safer just to stay away. Speaking of staying away from things, allow me to introduce you to payday loans.

The Good, The Bad And The Payday Loan

There are some things that you should just stay away from altogether. The payday loan is one of those things.

Payday Loan: A short-term loan that is lent at a high rate of interest to be paid back with funds from subsequent paychecks.

I like making a profit as much as the next guy, maybe even more. But payday loans just seem a little obscene. If you live in a decent neighborhood, you may not even have noticed that these types of businesses exist. They tend to be in low-income, urban areas and have a history of preying on the consumer who lives paycheck to paycheck.

Yes, I understand that payday loans are 100% voluntary and consumers don't have to use them if they don't want to. But I am simply playing the role of financial watchdog here.

I want readers to be aware of how dangerous these products are, so here are a few bullet points to help you understand how these products work:

- These are short-term loans payed out in cash
- Borrowers write a personal check PLUS the finance charge to get cash
- Borrowers authorize electronic access to their personal bank account
- Borrowers need a bank account, ID, and income stream
- A full credit check is usually not performed
- Borrowers are not fully vetted to determine ability to pay
- Annual percentage rates can easily reach 500-600%
- Borrowers default on 1 in 5 loans

Consider yourself warned.

Now What?

Are you already in a situation where you owe money that you are paying interest on each month? Credit cards, student loans, and car loans can strip you of your ability to build wealth. Eliminate your debt immediately and do not allow yourself to fall into that trap again. Let's take a look at how to do that in a short case study.

Meet Grace. Grace graduated from college 6 months ago, and her student loan repayment program has just begun. In addition to that, she has a car loan, a credit card, and an electric keyboard loan that she signed for through the local music store. Grace was recently able to land a job in her field of study and wants to start getting rid of her debt.

Grace's payments are as follows:

Type of Debt	Amount of Debt	Interest Rate
Car Loan	$3200	7.9%
Credit Card	$2350	25.79%
Student Loan	$32,000	5.7%
Keyboard Loan	$684	19.99%

I am going to show you the formula I use to pay off debt.

5 Steps To Eliminate Debt

Start by laying everything out in front of you in a chart similar to the one above. Use the form in this book (Appendix C) to proceed.

1. Separate the balances that are less than $1000.
2. Of those, IMMEDIATELY ATTACK THE DEBT WITH THE LOWEST AMOUNT. Use any money you have available to do this. Focus everything on this one debt until you have paid it off. You will pay the MINIMUM AMOUNT DUE on the remainder of your debts.
3. Once you have finished the first one, MOVE ON TO THE NEXT LOWEST one until you have paid off all of you debts under

$1000. You will continue to pay the minimum monthly payments on the remainder of your debts.
4. Next, FOCUS ON INTEREST RATES. Line up the remainder of your debts from highest to lowest in terms of the interest rates that you pay on them.
5. IMMEDIATELY ATTACK THE DEBT WITH THE HIGHEST INTEREST RATE and continue to pay the minimum monthly payments on the remainder of your debts.

Continue down the line until you have paid off all of your debts.

In Grace's case, she would begin by attacking the keyboard loan since that is the only balance under $1000. She would pay minimum payments on the rest of her debt. After she finished paying off the keyboard she would attack the credit card, since it has the highest interest rate. When that is paid, the car loan would be next on the list. Then, when she owned her car outright, she would only have the student loan remaining. Her debt repayment process would be complete when she finished attacking the student loan.

The amount you have available to pay your debts will be the same each month unless you start to make more money. However, by attacking each one separately, you are able to free up more money to attack with by eliminating payments as you go along.

I hope you can avoid the trap of debt altogether. However, if that is not the case, use this process to get rid of your debt as soon as possible. Having a plan to eliminate your debt is much better than the alternative of paying monthly payments as the interest continues to build and build and build.

Home Sweet Home

We all want the American dream, right? But should you pay for that dream for 30 years? That sounds like a nightmare to me. The 30-year mortgage was created to increase the size of the pool of people available to buy a home. Don't fall into that pool.

If you can't afford to buy a home on a 15-year fixed mortgage, you can't afford to buy a home. It should really be that simple. You don't deserve that debt. The difference in interest paid between a 15 and 30-year mortgage can be in the six-digits.

Resist the urge to have anything you want, whenever you want it. Stay away from credit cards; even if they say 0%. And if you do happen to have debt already, use the steps outlined here to pay it off immediately. Debt will follow you through life, taking away your ability to successfully build wealth. Don't allow yourself to be mediocre.

4.
Budgeting

"A budget is telling your money where to go instead of wondering where it went."

—*John C. Maxwell*

Do you have one of those friends on social media that posts about their upcoming vacation months in advance? I'm talking about the type of person that lets you know where they are going, what airline they are flying, what hotel they'll be staying at; you almost feel like you're going along with them. I never understood why we plan our vacations down to the minute, yet we just assume that someone else will plan our retirement.

SPOILER ALERT: NOBODY ELSE IS PLANNING IT!

Please take responsibility for yourself by creating a plan. The best way to start the planning process is by creating a budget. I have included a form (Appendix D) for you to begin - or you can go to www.greenaboutmoney.com/forms to download one for free.

All you need to do is fill in the blanks. You can do this!

Establishing A Budget

I have outlined several general expense categories in the 'Monthly Budget' form in this book (Appendix D). I have also included my recommendations as to how much I believe you should be allocating for each of these categories. Keep in mind that these are just recommendations. Each individual situation is unique.

We all have fixed costs in our lives that can be planned for such as housing, food, and transportation. We all need a place to live, food to eat, and a way to get from place to place. So plan for them. Most people don't have trouble with the fixed expenses due to the routine way in which they come about each month.

We also need to budget for our expenses that might not be the same every month; like perhaps your utilities or your phone bill. This is where a lot of people struggle. And before I had a budget, I struggled with this as well. See if what I do will work for you.

I take the bills that have variable payments, and I look at the last 6 to 12 months. Then I find the highest amount that I paid for each of them during that period and I use that number as my monthly budget for the next 6-12 months. This way I know I will be safe when it comes time to pay the bill. Any money you have left over can go into savings or flow into another budget category for that month.

The key point here is to assign a value to every area of your life that you either want or need money to go. If you don't tell your money where to go, nobody will. Remember, those who fail to plan, plan to fail. Let's take a closer look at each category.

Income

This category is simply how much money you make after taxes (your take-home pay). Include everything in this: your salary, your babysitting money, any money you get from relatives, etc. We don't discriminate here; the money all spends the same.

Housing

Recommended: 25%

To buy, or not to buy; that is the question. We all need a place to lay our head. The question becomes; 'Where are you in your life?' Have you been at your job longer than two years? Do you have any roots in the community? Are you close to family/friends?

My suggestion to most young people just starting out is to rent until they are at least 25. This is not a hard and fast rule, however. Keep your housing expenses as low as possible, 25% or below.

Buying

Buying a house is a big commitment. There can be a heavy burden placed on those who make the mistake of buying too early. Market prices can fluctuate and rates can change as well. If you aren't sure that you are ready, don't take the leap. Be very calculated about your decision. Stick to the 25% rule of your budget and that will make a lot of decisions for you.

If you are ready to buy, great. Just don't get trapped. What happens if you suddenly lose your job or you get transferred? Now, instead of your house being your largest asset, the property has become a major liability. Don't get stuck with a mortgage that you can't afford when a major life event decides to slap you in the face.

I bought my first house when I was 21, but the average age of a first-time home buyer in 2015 was 33 years old.[2] You won't be left behind if you don't buy in your 20's.

Renting

Since the financial crisis of 2008, the percentage of people who rent their home has increased substantially. In 2006, the percentage of renters between the age of 18-34 years old was 62.5%. In 2014, that number jumped to 71.6% according to Trulia.com.[3]

Keep in mind that if you can keep your housing costs low, you are going to be off to a great start. This is the highest percentage category for most people. You could really make some headway on paying down debt or saving for a home later in life if you can keep your housing costs low while you are young.

Conversely, I see way too many people today wanting to live in a trendy, urban location. If you are paying more than 25% of your housing

---

[2] Search Results. (2017). National Mortgage Professional Magazine. Retrieved from http://nationalmortgageprofessional.com/news/55433/zillow-average-first-timehomebuyer-33-years-age

[3] Uh, M. (2017). From Own To Rent: Who Lost The American Dream? - Trulia's Blog. Trulia's Blog. Retrieved from https://www.trulia.com/blog/trends/own-to-rent/

allotment, you can't afford it. I don't care how close to the coffee shop it happens to be; stick to that rule. If you find that story all too familiar, and you are in that situation right now, get out immediately and lower that payment.

Transportation

Recommended: 12%

This may be difficult, but try to resist the temptation to buy that sports car or luxury vehicle right out of the gate. There will be plenty of time for that later in life when you have a stronger financial foothold. Even if you do manage to be able to afford the vehicle of your dreams (or even a loan for it), you will most likely get swallowed up by high insurance rates and registration costs. And we haven't even talked about the fuel costs yet. You may not turn any heads driving that 15-year-old hand-me-down, but the money you save will be worth it later on.

Vehicles are a depreciating asset. That means they are one of the worst investments you can make. I use the word 'investment' extremely loosely here. No matter what a car dealer tells you about the great resale value a potential vehicle has, it is still like picking the best tomato out of the bunch. Eventually, it turns rotten.

Another form of transportation that has become increasingly popular as of late is ridesharing. Companies such as Uber and Lyft have seen incredible growth in the young demographic industry. If you don't need a vehicle and can complement ridesharing with public transportation, you could really be in the driver's seat. Just remember to plan your budget accordingly if you are using this type of transportation and be aware of any price changes during peak hours.

Savings/Investments

Recommended: 15%

Save 15% of ALL money you earn. If there's only one thing in this book that you do, please do this. Save more if you can, but make 15% the minimum. You will see why we do this in later chapters. Do not steal from this category to buy a round of drinks for your friends. You will only be stealing from yourself.

Food

Recommended: 12%

This category alone could save you thousands of dollars per year. Investors Business Daily put out an article in September of 2016 citing the divergence of the cost of eating out versus eating in. They found that fast food prices had risen 6% in the two years prior while the cost of eating at home had actually fallen 1%.[4]

If you plan right, you can hit the 12% mark easily. In fact, you can probably aim for 10% if you are eating your meals at home. Stop eating out. There are much better ways to spend your money. More on this topic in the next chapter.

---

[4] GRAHAM, J. (2017). Off The Charts: Fast Food Inflation Vs. Eating In. Investor's Business Daily. Retrieved from http://www.investors.com/news/economy/this-rise-in-fast-food-prices-vs-eating-in-costs-is-off-the-charts/

Debt

Recommended: 9%

This is only for people that have debt (probably most of you). If you don't, however, add 5% more to your saving and allocate the rest accordingly. For the majority of you, get rid of your debt immediately. Use the 'Eliminate Your Debt' form and write down all of your debt. When paying them off, the 9% recommended mark should be your minimum. Spend whatever you need to in this category to decrease the size of your debt.

Utilities

Recommended: 8%

I think 8% on utilities is actually a little high, but they vary so much from state to state that I wanted to err on the high side. You're always going to be paying for utilities in some form or fashion. It is simply one of those cost of living expenses that never really goes away unless you happen to live off the grid.

Insurance/Medical

Recommended: 7%

This is one of those categories that you should not feel bad about spending money in. That is, of course, assuming you have good insurance. Having good insurance is important in almost every category, whether it be Health, Auto or Life. Be sure to get more than one opinion when shopping for insurance.

Personal

Recommended: 7%

The personal category can include anything from toiletries to clothing. These are the expenses that come up from time to time that you need to remember to plan for. This is a category that will be pretty flexible. So if you don't spend your allotment for the month, be sure to carry it over to the next month so you aren't cut short. You never know when you're gonna get a hole in your sock.

Entertainment

Recommended: 5%

I want to talk briefly about spending money on entertainment. Typically, younger generations are going to spend more (strictly on a percent basis) than most in this category. I don't necessarily think that is a bad thing, but don't go overboard. Don't turn it into a license to spend.

It's hard to put a price tag on the most memorable events in our lives. Whether that experience was traveling with a group of friends or seeing your favorite band when they came to town, memorable life events are important to have. It never makes sense to use debt to finance them, however.

The key is to find a balance when accounting for your monthly expenses. Make sure you budget for the Saturday nights just as you do for the Monday nights.

I Love It When A Plan Comes Together

So now you have your budget. Can you live with it? Do you see where you can start cutting your expenses and bank some of those savings? Are you adding up all the money you spent going out to eat last month? It's pretty brutal when you lay everything out in front of you. But that is exactly what you need at this point in your life; brutal honesty.

If you can have the discipline to pass on the new car and walk past the trendy apartment with a bag lunch in your hand, your future is going to look pretty bright. Stick to your new budget like your life depends on it; because it does.

5.
SPENDING

"Don't tell me where your priorities are. Show me where you spend your money and I'll tell you what they are."

—James W. Frick

I'm gonna let you in on a little secret: it doesn't matter how much money you make. If you spend more money than you take in, you will eventually be broke.

I once met someone at a job I was working for the summer that had absolutely no idea how to handle money. We were paid every Friday, and every Friday this person would act like a sailor on leave as soon as he got his paycheck. He would spend money on the stupidest things. Then, come Monday morning, he would beg people for a cigarette and complain how broke he was.

Can you see how foolish that is? We have a spending problem in the United States. Society tells us that we can have anything we want, and we are foolish enough to believe it. It's time to wake up and realize that our actions have consequences. Don't be held captive by the credit card companies your entire life. You don't deserve that. Start good spending habits while you're young and let's break the chain of careless spending in America.

Straight Cash

'Cash is King'. Drill that into your brain. You should get to a point where all you have is one debit card and some cash in your pocket. Because here's the thing about cash: you can't overdraft. If you don't have any, you can't spend any. And that's a huge part of the problem with having a card in your pocket. You never really know what your balance is at any given point in time.

I started a concessions business when I was 21 years old. I had two mobile concession stands that I would take to festivals and fairs around my home state. I honestly can't think of another business that could have taught me the basics of money and economics better than that business did. After the fifth year of operation, it felt like a finely-tuned machine.

I did not accept credits cards; the business was straight cash. And at some events, I took in a lot of cash. Well, a lot for someone my age at least. The mindset is just so much different in that situation. When you hold money in your hand versus swiping a card or writing a check, you are much more careful about how that money is spent. It isn't just a number on a screen at that point. It is tangible.

So how do you apply that to your life? Well, for the money that you spend on groceries, gas, and entertainment; use cash. You can stick to your budget much more easily when you take money out of your account for specific purchases each month. And my guess is that you will spend less when you do that as well. Speaking of spending less; did you know that there are places where you can actually get a discount for paying in cash versus paying by card?

I personally know of an auto service shop that will offer a discount on service for things such as oil changes and other regular maintenance. And there are gas stations (especially truck stops) that will offer a cash price for fuel. How about when you go to purchase a car? If you show up with hundred dollar bills, I guarantee you will get some extra attention from a salesperson willing to close the sale.

So ask for a cash discount when you go places. Will people think that is tacky? I doubt it, but who cares? As a business owner, I can tell you that I would definitely not be offended for any reason by someone asking for a cash discount. You can build relationships with people by establishing a dialogue as well, which never hurts. So what does it hurt to ask?

Why are they willing to offer a discount in the first place? The main reason is because it is not free to have credit card companies process transactions. Business owners pay a percentage of the sale to the credit card company when they charge a customer's card. This can be anywhere from 1% to 3%. And on smaller transactions, they may even pay a fixed price plus a percentage.

Another less common reason to prefer a cash transaction is the threat of a chargeback.

Chargeback: The return of funds to an account from the merchant, typically after a dispute on a transaction.

The bottom line is that business owners understand the costs of doing business associated with credit cards. So, many companies build those costs into the price of an item. So if it makes sense to eliminate that cost for any reason, you may just end up saving yourself some money.

What's In Your Pocket?

Reach into your pocket. What's inside? I'm sure most of you will say your driver's license, maybe some cash, or a bank card or two. Perhaps all you have is your phone. Technology is simplifying our lives in many ways, and banks are among those leading the way. The way we pay for things is constantly evolving. However, the concept of money, and how it works, remains the same.

I walk into Starbucks most mornings carrying only my phone. Their app allows me to scan a barcode (on my phone) that is linked to my personal account that I set up on their system. That account acts like a holding tank for the money that I use specifically at Starbucks. When the balance runs low, I simply allocate more funds by reloading the account via a debit card that I have saved on the app. I can also add money by paying cash at a register in a store. It's a simple and easy-to-use system.

With that technology, however, I have to be disciplined and remember to keep track of my spending. Because no matter what type of platform that is used, I still need money to pay for things at the end of the day. Now, I'm just a black coffee drinker, so the costs are minimal in comparison to some of the fancier drinks there, but the costs still add up. If I don't plan for those purchases, I could wind up being short of money that I need in another area.

Are You A Subscriber?

Beware of little expenses; a small leak will sink a great ship."

—*Benjamin Franklin*

Who doesn't love 'easy'? You can pretty much get anything delivered right to your doorstep these days. God bless the internet, right? Businesses understand that customers gravitate to products and services with ecosystems that are easy to adapt to. One way companies use to keep consumers loyal is through subscriptions.

Netflix is one of the most popular subscription-based services on the market right now; I love it. Consumers pay a monthly fee and have access to their entire catalog of movies and shows. The company has simplified their sign-up process to where almost anyone could figure it out and start enjoying the content.

They make it easy because they know that once you get in, you won't want to quit. In your mind, it seems like such a minimal cost that it won't make too much of a dent in your bank account each month. That's when they have you.

Subscriptions are popping up everywhere now from razor blades to dog food. People are moving toward simplicity and ease-of-use. My warning to you is to really consider whether you need that subscription or not. Because if it's just another thing that is taking $10 from you every month, your retirement fund will be the real loser in the long run.

How Would You Like That Prepared?

"Before anything else, preparation is the key to success."
—Alexander Graham Bell

When I started truly controlling how I spent money, I knew I was going to have a problem with how I spent money in relation to food. I love going out to eat. I love trying new restaurants and visiting local favorites. The problem, however, is that most young people cannot afford to eat out. And I'm including fast food in that.

If you have any type of debt whatsoever, you should not be going out to eat. For some people to rein in spending, all they need to do is start preparing their meals at home and they will literally save thousands of dollars. It's just too expensive versus buying groceries and preparing your meals at home. If you don't believe me, add up all of your meals that were eaten out in the past month and then grab your credit card statement. Did you spend $100, $200, $300? What if, instead, you had used that money to pay down your debt?

'BUT I DON'T HAVE ENOUGH TIME'! False. You need to make the time. Take a couple of hours on Sunday to prepare your meals for the week. You don't need to actually make them, but plan what you are going to have each day and make sure you have the ingredients all ready to go. First of all, this will relieve the stress of having to figure out what you are going to eat each day. And second, you will have a plan that you can stick to when you drive by that taco place on the way home from work.

A single person can get by on $75-$100 per week on food if you shop responsibly and prepare your meals at home. That should come out to about 10%-15% of your monthly income. You just cannot expect to get ahead if you are spending more than that in this category.

Give yourself a crash course on meal preparation. You can turn on the Food Network (if you have cable) to get ideas, or just search for recipes online. You will probably end up eating healthier and spending much less on food if you do this.

And for the times when you do allow yourself to go out, like for a friend's birthday or a celebration, I guarantee you will appreciate the experience much more knowing that you have planned for it in your budget.

Live Below Your Means

It's Saturday night. Your friends are going out to grab something to eat before dropping by a new club that just opened up downtown. Do you: A) Join in, B) Skip dinner and meet them at the club, or C) Make dinner and binge watch Netflix?

The truth is, living below your means will get you so much farther ahead than trying to live in a world that you can't afford. Spending less money than you take in is the basis of fundamental economics. I understand why people don't do this, however.

It's difficult to say 'no.' You might feel like you are missing out on things. And you very well might be. But you cannot keep spending money that you do not have. That's why so many Americans are in the financial position they are in. They can't say 'no.' They have to keep up appearances. They have to buy the newest "whatever." The neighbors got a new car, why can't I? I deserve it...

And there lies the problem. Why do you deserve it? Do you deserve to be in debt? Will you deserve it later in life when you become a ward of the state because you ran out of money and now have to rely on the government to take care of you? I do not wish that on you.

Far too many people that drive that new car or buy that new "whatever" are living a lie. Resist the temptation of living a gotta-have-it life. Live below your means now, and enjoy life like crazy when you are actually able to.

Missed Opportunity

Opportunity manifests itself in many different forms. Some of them, however, are never even seen by us. I am about to tell you about a concept that changed the way I looked at how I spent money. Allow me to introduce you to the concept of opportunity cost.

Opportunity Cost: The money or benefit an individual could have received, but lost, due to following another course of action.

In 2002, I bought a brand new truck. I ordered it with all the options and since I got low-interest financing, I was convinced that I had done the right thing. I was able to get tax deductions because I used it for business and it made traveling a lot more fun. But I admit that I had some buyer's remorse after the deal was done. I felt like I was missing something.

What I was missing out on were all the ways I could have used that money differently. Let me give you an example: In January of 2002 (when I bought the truck), the technology company Apple was trading at a price of $1.50 per share (split-adjusted). Let's say that I put $10,000 down on the truck as a down payment in January (I don't know the exact figure). If instead of using that $10,000 on the truck, I used it to buy Apple stock, I could have purchased 6,666 shares at that point in time.

Hindsight is 20/20. I no longer have that truck. I do, however, have the aching in my gut at what I could have owned instead. Apple is now trading at roughly $143 per share. At today's price, my 6,666 shares of stock would be worth $953,238. Basically $1 million. That, my friends, is opportunity cost.

This is a difficult topic for many people. Too many Americans fail to have the discipline necessary to control their spending. So instead of building wealth, they build debt. We need to break that cycle. Pay in cash, be diligent about your eating habits, and just generally live below your means. Be smart with your money and may all the opportunities you miss out on be worthless.

6.
Saving

"The habit of saving is itself an education; it fosters every virtue, teaches self-denial, cultivates the sense of order, trains to forethought, and so broadens the mind."

—T.T. Munger

A penny saved is a penny earned. Does that sound old-fashioned to you? Well, it's a very old saying, so it should. But no matter how old the saying, I believe there is value there. I'm going to be blunt with you; you won't get rich overnight. You can, however, build tremendous wealth by instituting a calculated savings plan that includes the strategies outlined in this chapter.

The U.S. Personal Savings Rate has been trending downward since the mid 1970's. This rate calculates the amount of disposable income that is saved by individuals. Add to that the increasing average amount of debt that American citizens have, and you can start to see the major problem that exists.

So here is what you need to do. It's really very simple. You need to start saving money. Make it so automatic that you don't even think about. I've outlined two very basic steps for you on the next page.

Step Two It

STEP 1: The first step in saving is to reach a balance in your bank account of at least $500. Once you do that, DO NOT touch it unless it's an emergency. Never let that balance drop below $500. Some call this an emergency fund and others call it a buffer strategy. Whatever you call it, leave it alone. Its sole purpose is to be there when you need it. And you'll know when that is. Some sweltering day in August you'll be driving along and start to see steam coming out from under the hood of your car. That's when you'll be thankful you have that money. If you deplete that money, make sure to put it all back for the next time life knocks on your door.

STEP 2: Next, start saving at least 15% of your income as of your next paycheck. Then never stop. Ever. If you have an employer, you will be doing this through your 401k (or 403b if you are employed by a school or other tax-exempt organizations). If you are self-employed, or your employer does not offer a 401k, you will be doing this through an IRA. This commitment to saving 15% of your income will prove to be one of your GREATEST achievements later in life. Trust me, you will thank me later. Saving is an absolute necessity if you want to build wealth.

Habit-Forming

"Good habits formed at youth make all the difference."

—Aristotle

I recently started a morning exercise routine. It's important for you to understand how much I loathe the act of exercising in order for you to really appreciate this analogy. I knew that I needed to start doing something for exercise. So after writing out the goal, I made a conscious decision in my mind that I was going to start.

I purchased an elliptical machine for my home because I found that getting a gym membership does not work for me. For one, the subscription model of a gym membership was taking away money that I could use more effectively in other areas. And two, I just couldn't get myself to take the time to go.

So I paid the one-time fee for this machine that now sits in my living room as a daily reminder. It has been in my home for three months now, and for three months I have made it a point to spend the first 30 minutes of my day listening to the morning financial news while using my new elliptical machine.

I won't lie, the first two weeks were hard. I used a lot of willpower to get on that thing. The general consensus is that it takes 21 days to form a habit. I can tell you that I probably used up the entire 21 days; but I did it. I am feeling better now and I'm also noticing the other benefits that come from incorporating exercise into your daily routine as well.

I'm telling you this story in an attempt to say to you: 'you can do it.' If I can get into the habit of exercising every day, you can start saving money. It might not be easy, but the good things that come to you in life hardly ever are. Start with a manageable goal, and proceed from there. Make it a habit to succeed. Your life will be changed in so many ways.

Where Else Do I Save?

Bank accounts are definitely not the only place you should be saving your money. In fact, once you have your emergency fund in place, you should be focusing on these next options to take you into the second stage of saving.

401(k)

401(k) Plan: A retirement savings plan established by companies that allow employees to contribute earned income through salary-reduction on a pre-tax basis.

If your employer offers a 401(k) (and most do), you should absolutely enroll. I cannot stress this enough. This will be your main savings vehicle that will bring you into retirement. Each year, the IRS sets a contribution limit for all taxpayers no matter how much money you make. For 2017, the contribution limit remained at $18,000.

What this means is that, for the entire year of 2017, you can withhold up to $18,000 from your paycheck on a pre-tax basis (before you pay taxes on it). This reduces your overall taxable income, thus reducing the amount of taxes that you will owe for the year. Sounds pretty great, huh?

Let's go a step further into the 401(k) plan and talk about free money. Interested? You better be! Within a 401(k) savings plan is an option for employers to MATCH employee contributions up to a certain percentage. Now, not all employers will match funds, but most large companies will. Typically, this percentage ranges from 3% to 6%.

So let's say that you have elected to contribute 15% of your income to your 401(k) plan (like I told you to). If your employer matches contributions up to 5%, that money will automatically get invested along with your contributions without you having to lift a finger. That's like getting a 5% raise for doing nothing but saving for retirement! Make it a point to max out your 401(k) every year and cash in on the savings.

To get enrolled in your company's 401(k) plan, start by looking at these general steps:

STEP 1: Talk to your human resources department to find out who handles your company's retirement accounts. Your H/R representative will most likely be a great asset in helping you do this. Two examples of companies that your employer might work with are Paychex and Fidelity, but there are many more.

STEP 2: Gather all of your relevant employee information. You will need this when you get to the website of the company that is handling your 401(k). It is possible you will need your employee number or start date to verify your employment with them (in addition to your personal information such as SSN and birthdate).

STEP 3: Once you are on their website, start the process of enrollment by following their prompts. If you have any trouble with anything along the way, be sure to contact their customer service department.

STEP 4: Once your account is setup, you will need to direct your contributions to specific types of investments. This process will vary substantially from company to company. Many 401(k) savings plans will have target retirement dates that you can reference. For instance, if you turn 65 in the year 2065, you might want to look at the 2065 target date. Your goal here is be invested somewhere other than just cash so you can obtain growth in your portfolio. Talk to a financial professional for help on where to invest.

IRA (Traditional)

Individual Retirement Account: A type of tax-advantaged investment account that allows individuals to save for retirement on a tax-deferred basis.

If you are an average person just out of college right now, you will have about 3 to 4 job changes by the time you are 30 years old. The significance of that lies in the number of retirement accounts you will have at the end of that time. If you take my advice and get a 401(k) at each of those jobs, you will then have 4 separate retirement accounts you have to maintain. There is a way you can avoid the hassle of maintaining these, individually.

Find a reputable investment bank where you feel comfortable setting up an IRA. Most large banks these days have their own in-house investment banks. So if you already bank with a large financial institution, you can simply ask them to set up a Traditional IRA for you. There should no fee associated with doing this. In fact, many banks now pay YOU to put your money with them in the form of sign-up bonuses.

Once you have an IRA established, plan on keeping it for the long haul. Because for every job change that you have, you will have a lonely 401(k) with no money going into it anymore. The way we solve that problem is by transferring the funds in that 401(k) to your IRA. This process is called a rollover.

Rollover: *The transfer of financial assets from one retirement plan to another without tax penalties.*

More specifically, the process most of you will be performing will be a 'direct' rollover. This just means that you will have no contact with the money, yourself. The funds will go 'directly' from your 401(k) to your IRA, electronically. Be aware of any tax consequences (each situation is unique, so speak to a tax professional if you have any questions on this).

Now that you have funds in your IRA, you have much more freedom in where you invest as opposed to the types of restrictions placed by the companies that maintained your 401(k). Just make sure you understand all the fees associated with trading in that account (again with the fees). If you are a novice investor, you shouldn't be making very many trades anyway. Always keep your target retirement date in mind.

Now, if by chance you turn out to be one of those people who ends up LOVING the first job that you get out of college and never have any job changes… You should still open up a traditional IRA because of the tax benefits associated with them. As of this year (2017), the contributions you make (up to $5000) can be tax deductible. I believe you should take advantage of all the avenues you have available to you when preparing for retirement.

ROTH IRA

ROTH IRA: An individual retirement account that allows investors to use after-tax money to save for retirement and benefit from tax-free withdrawals after a predetermined age.

Are you someone that worries about the future? Are you afraid that one day your taxes might be so high that you have to give up huge chunks to Uncle Sam when it comes time for you to pull money out of your retirement fund? Then the Roth IRA might be just what you are looking for.

As mentioned above, the Roth IRA allows you to deposit after-tax money (money that has already been taxed). The benefit here comes at the time you retire. When it comes time for you to pull that money out, your withdrawals come out tax-free. So you don't have to worry what tax rates will be at that time. The hard part is done, and that can give people a lot of peace of mind.

Consider opening up a Roth IRA and funding it with any 'extra' money you might have. Have a second job? Fund your Roth. Finish paying your car payment? Use the extra money that you're not paying on that to fund your Roth. It's yet another way we have to build wealth in the United States and allow our 'future selves' the opportunity to really live.

Brokerage Account

Brokerage Account: A type of investment account that is set up between a licensed brokerage firm and investor, typically for the purchase of stocks or exchange-traded funds (ETF's).

To simplify that definition, a brokerage account is where you can buy and sell stocks of publicly traded companies. This is simply the vehicle you can use to accomplish your saving goals. We will talk more about the various products you can buy and sell with a brokerage account in the coming chapter on investing.

As with other types of accounts, be sure to examine the fees associated with this account. Most brokerage accounts will charge a fee every time you place a trade with them. This includes both buying and selling. If you plan on doing a lot of trading, be sure to find a broker with low trading fees. An example of this type of broker would be a 'discount broker.'

Discount Broker: A type of stockbroker who charges a lower fee for investment orders than a typical full-service broker.

If you save 15% of every paycheck from now until retirement, you will be way ahead of your peers. Will that be enough money for you? It all depends on how lavish you want your retirement years to be. Use your 401k to start building a massive amount of wealth on a tax-deferred basis. Then incorporate the other methods we discussed as well. You will be unstoppable! Start these good habits now while you are young. They will make all the difference.

7.
INTERESTING

"My wealth has come from a combination of living in America, some lucky genes, and compound interest"

—*Warren Buffett*

Have you ever wondered how rich people get to where they are? Yes, there is a percentage of wealthy people who were born into money. A larger percentage build wealth by hard work and determination. And then there's the x-factor: compound interest.

Compound Interest: Interest that is calculated on both the initial principal and any accrued interest.

In the most simplistic form, this is money going out and making more money. When you get your money working for you, you will find that it will continuously find more money recruits to help in the process. This, in turn, makes your money 'army' bigger and stronger. The more money you have, the more money you could potentially make. And this process goes on and on.

To explain this concept further, let's say you received $1000 from your family for graduation. Most of you are probably going to use that toward tuition costs or some basic living needs. What if, instead of spending it, you invested it? Humor me here. Let's say that you just happened to hear that a particular mutual fund was averaging 10% per year for the last 20 years. So you decide to invest your $1000 into that fund.

A year later as you're flipping through your mail, you happen to notice an envelope. You open it up and see that it is the annual results of your mutual fund performance. You look at the bottom of the page and notice that your balance is now $1100. You made 10% on your investment in the past year. Feeling happy, you decide to keep that money invested for another year. Only now, your balance is $100 more than last year.

Another year passes, and you open up your statement again. You are delighted to see that your balance has increased to $1210. Do you see what happened? You made $10 more this year ($110 total for the year) just because your beginning balance was $100 more than the previous year. You can see how that will eventually go, right?

The next five years will be $1331, $1464.10, 1610.51, $1771.56 and $1948.71, respectively. That's assuming you just leave the account alone. So in 7 years, you essentially doubled your money. If you left that money alone for 50 years (basically until you retired), you would have $117,390.85. Are you sure you want to spend that money on toilet paper and rent?

To harness the power of compound interest effectively, you need time. Give me time and money and I will show you the time of your life.

Now imagine what would happen if you decide to continue to fund your investment with every paycheck that you receive. Remember when I talked about saving 15% of your income? This is when it gets fun.

$0 to WHAT?!

Remember Grace from Chapter 3: *Borrowing*? The 22-year-old had just graduated from college and landed a job for herself. We came up with a plan for her to start paying off her debt. Our next step in helping Grace down her path to retirement is to carry out a financial forecast for her.

With the aid of a retirement calculator, we will be entering in some basic information to give us an idea of how much money she will have when she retires. Find a retirement calculator (Bankrate.com has a good one) and do the same for yourself as we go along.

We start by inputting some basic data points. All we are doing here is entering in some information that pertains to you and your job. Here is what Grace entered:

401k Employee Savings Plan:	
Percent to Contribute	15%
Annual Salary	$40,000
Annual Salary Increase	2%
Current Age	22
Age of Retirement	65
Current 401(k) Balance	$0
Annual Rate of Return	10%

As you can see, Grace started out with nothing ($0) in her 401(k) since she just started her job. She plans on contributing 15% of her annual $40,000 salary. Her company averages 3% salary increases per year, however, we stayed conservative and only entered 2%. She is 22 years old and plans to retire at 65.

The only other thing we need to know is the annual rate of return she expects to get over the life of her investments. We entered 10% here since that is a relatively conservative estimate of returns based upon the history of the U.S. stock market.

401(k) Employer Match	
Employer Match	100%
Employer Match Up To	4%

In this section, we are asked about how Grace's company deals with 401(k) matching funds. Her company matches 100% of the amount she invests up to 4% of her total income. Grace can invest more than that, however, the company will not match anything over 4%. Let's take a look at the results of Grace's retirement calculator.

The Results

Grace, 22 years old, started with $0 in her account. With an annual salary of $40,000 and an annual salary increase of 2%, she expects a 10% return. Grace is contributing 15% of her income and her employer matches 100% of that money up to 4%. Here is what she will end up with at age 65 according to the retirement calculator:

- With employer match: $5,793,788
- Without employer match: $4,574,045

Retirement calculators should only be used as self-help guides, and not as a means of replacing expert financial advice. Always consult a professional for any questions you may have regarding your individual investment needs.

Can you start to see how these numbers increase over time? It starts to become unstoppable near her retirement age. The two results that are shown are $5.7 million (that includes her employer's matching funds) and $4.5 million (the amount she would have if her employer did not match. That is the power of compound interest and time. Now imagine if you did this making $80,000 per year.

If you have access to a 401(k) and are not contributing to it, start immediately. This is a phenomenal way to start benefitting from compound interest. Take advantage of your youth and give your money the time it needs to start growing into a massive amount of wealth.

Did you know you could actually lose money over time if you only put your money in a savings account? This is explained by the concept of inflation.

Inflation

"Inflation is the one form of taxation that can be imposed without legislation."

—Milton Friedman

Inflation: The rise in the general level of prices resulting in the fall in value of a currency.

The 1970's were a tough time for America as a nation. As our country was reaching it's bicentennial, we were fighting a real war abroad and a financial war at home. Interest rates were skyrocketing along with the price of gas. Inflation had arrived and was punching everyone in the stomach.

I left you dangling in the last section by saying you could lose money by keeping money in your checking account, so allow me to explain. According to Bankrate.com, the interest rate you receive on a checking account today is 0.43%. Along with that, the current inflation rate is 2.7%.

Do you see where this is going? If we just want to break even on our money, we need to make 2.7% (current inflation). But we are only making 0.43%. So that means we are actually losing 2.27% of our money each year that this trend continues (Interest-Inflation). This is called the real interest rate.

Real Interest Rate: The rate an investor expects to receive after factoring the effects of inflation.

Let's think about fast food for a minute. Remember when the 'Dollar Menu' actually consisted of food that cost $1? That's how it started, of course. Now, you can hardly find anything for $1 that isn't a miniaturized version of its former self. The current 'Value Menu' includes items for $2, $3 and even $4 in price. That is a common example of inflation; items that used to cost less than they do now.

So how do we know when we are experiencing inflation? How is it measured? The U.S. government, through the U.S. Bureau of Labor Statistics, publishes a monthly gauge of inflation called the Consumer Price Index (CPI).

Consumer Price Index (CPI): An index that measures the change in price of a basket of goods and services.

Remember when we set up our budgets in Chapter 4? Most of the things in your budget are included in the consumer price index. It essentially states how much it costs to live. Now, you don't necessarily need to keep track of the monthly CPI numbers, but it is important to understand the concept since it relates directly to your money and finances.

I hope you found this chapter 'interesting.' You don't need to be rich, or even make a lot of money, to retire comfortably. Grace proved that. With her modest $40,000 per year salary, Grace will be prepared to enjoy life and even have enough money to manage if she runs into a few bumps along the road (like inflation). This is so easy, people. You can do this. Interested?

8.
INVESTING

"The individual investor should act consistently as an investor and not as a speculator."

—Ben Graham

I started following the financial markets at a fairly young age. I actually find it quite fascinating. I could (and many days do) watch financial news all day long. The financial markets are all about 'possibility' to me. They give the everyday person the option to have a chip in the game.

You don't have to have a million dollar net worth to invest in the stock market. Take a look at Apple for instance. The technology company has seen their stock essentially go from $1 to $136 in just the last 14 years (split-adjusted). You can take part in situations like that. Publicly-traded companies are just waiting for new capital. Take a look at Facebook. That social media stock has had a massive run up in price in just the last few years. Now, they aren't all going to be winners like those two, but read this quote from the legendary Wayne Gretzky:

"You miss 100% of the shots you don't take."

—Wayne Gretzky

Start with a small amount of money and find some investments to get involved in. You can even find a virtual trading account to start with. Many brokerage companies have practice accounts you can use to start trading with before you use real money. This is a great way to start learning the process.

Getting Started

"An investment in knowledge pays the best interest"

—Benjamin Franklin

At the time I am writing this, Snap (the parent company of Snapchat) has just released their IPO (initial public offering).

Initial Public Offering (IPO): The first stock offering of a company to the public.

Snapchat currently captures (no pun intended) a large percentage of the coveted 18-34 year old demographic. The company has turned into a juggernaut. Perhaps, with companies like this going public, it will get the younger generation learning more about the investing process.

Do you want to invest in companies and brands that you already know are great ideas? Do you wish you had a chance to buy Apple 15 years ago? Get going by taking some easy steps that will put you in the position to find the next big thing.

We're just going to touch on the basics of investing here. I want to give you enough information to have an intelligent conversation with someone you meet in a coffee shop, but not so much that you close this book in sheer boredom.

There are plenty of books on the subject of investing that you can delve into if you decide you want to learn more. Check out Benjamin Graham's *The Intelligent Investor* if you are that person. Mr. Graham mentored Warren Buffett, so you might want to listen to what he has to say.

The majority of people who are invested in the financial markets do so through securities.

Security: A financial instrument such as stocks or bonds that can be traded in the market.

Stocks

"Stocks allow the average individual a way to beat the averages."
—Jeff Tarman

Stock: A financial security that signifies an ownership relationship to a company.

Stocks garner the majority of the interest of individual investors. The reason has to do with the familiarity with their respective companies and the opportunity for price appreciation. Investors have built tremendous amounts of wealth in the U.S. stock market.

The S&P 500 is a stock index of 500 large companies traded in the United States. It gives a glimpse at how the American economy is doing at a particular moment in time. This index is filled with companies that most people would be familiar with such as Home Depot, Google and McDonald's.

Average people come into contact with these corporations on a frequent basis and they could probably give you a reason as to why they would want to invest money with them or not. It isn't too difficult to understand the business model of McDonald's.

If consumers believe that McDonald's is increasing sales (selling more hamburgers) and gaining market share (taking customers from another burger chain) in the fast food industry, it would be natural for them to want to purchase shares of their stock. Doing so gives them ownership in the company as well as the ability to benefit from any growth in the company. Plus, it's kind of cool that you can say that you own part of McDonald's, right?

There are two things you want to know when talking about the stock of particular company: their price and their earnings. The price is simply the current price at which the stock is trading at any given point in time. Earnings are essentially the profit of a company.

Earnings: The profit of a company displayed as after-tax net income.

There is a ratio that investors use to get a glimpse of how a particular stock is being valued in the market called the Price to Earnings (P/E) Ratio.

Price-Earnings (P/E) Ratio: A ratio that values a company based on the company's share price in relation to their earnings per share.

When investing in stocks, the individual investor is looking for stocks with the capability of providing capital appreciation.

Capital Appreciation: An increase in the price of an asset.

You have most likely heard the phrase: Buy Low, Sell High. That is essentially how you accomplish the goal of capital appreciation. However, knowing when to sell is never easy. The key is to continually reassess the company based on facts, not emotion.

Stocks rise and fall in price due to many factors, but the major reason has to do with their earnings. Before the iPhone, Apple was mainly a computer company. But only a small percentage of people had their computers. Then Steve Jobs created the iPod, and subsequently the iPhone, and the company's earnings took off along with their stock price.

Again, stocks can go up and down in value. Stock prices can fluctuate with current market conditions. In a 'Bull Market,' the overall market is moving up in value. Conversely, a 'Bear Market' occurs when the overall market is trending downward.

When you buy stock, you are buying shares in that company.

Shares: An equal ownership unit of a company.

The key thing to remember about stocks is that you have an ownership relationship with the company. Bonds are the flip side of stocks.

Bonds

Bond: A debt instrument in which an entity pays interest to the certificate holder (investor) at a predetermined rate of interest and length of time.

I probably don't have to tell you that the bond market is not as exciting as the stock market (think paint drying). But investing is not always sexy and glamorous. Guaranteed returns (like from bonds) make for a stable, balanced portfolio of investments.

The key point to remember about the relationship between an investor and a company that issues a bond is that the investment is one of debt.

Mutual Funds

Mutual Fund: An investment product that pools the funds of investors and invests them in stocks, bonds, and other types of assets.

We touched on mutual funds previously when talking about 401(k) plans. As defined above, mutual funds are a group of different assets. Thus, by definition, they are more diversified. Therefore, the general public tends to view them as a safer way to be invested. However, always keep in mind that risk assets such as stocks, bonds, and mutual funds can go down just as fast as they go up. Do your research on where you invest your money.

Annuities

Annuity: A type of investment that builds up incremental cash value and then pays out those funds, plus any earned interest, to the annuitant or individual account holder.

There are many different types of annuities, so we are going to keep this as simple as possible. There are relatively safe types of annuities (such as fixed annuities) and there are annuities that carry more risk (such as variable annuities).

There are two phases of an annuity: Accumulation and Annuitization.

Accumulation Phase: A period of time when the value of an annuity is being built up by the investor.
Annuitization Phase: A period of time when the annuitant receives payments from the annuity.

The steady cash flow during the annuitization phase is why you own annuities. Investors in these products usually want a solid, reliable income stream for defined periods of time such as during retirement. Consider investing in annuities if you are looking for this type of investment.

Risky Business

If ever there was a time to take some financial risk, it would when you are young. The likelihood of you needing to access your money early in life is probably low, so if you have a propensity toward risk, get it out of your system early. I'm not saying you should do this with all of your money. That is never a good idea. A general rule of investing is to never allocate more than 20% of your money toward one investment.

This does not mean throwing caution to the wind, though. You still need to do your homework. The kinds of things I am talking about would be finding a Biotech company with a drug in the trial stages or investing seed money into tech startup run by investors with a proven track record. You have some time to be wrong if things don't go as planned. Just make sure you are on track with the rest of your portfolio.

Portfolio: *A group of financial holdings that include cash, stocks and other securities.*

Are You Diversified?

The only investors who shouldn't diversify are those who are right 100% of the time."

—John Templeton

Growing up in a small town, I had free reign to hit the streets come October 31st. The savagely means by which my friends and I gathered Halloween candy was truly a sight to behold. At the end of the night, the pillowcase full of sugary treats had to be a nightmare to any dentist alive.

One of the benefits of hitting so many houses was the final assortment of candy that we ended up with. From candy bars to suckers, and even the dreaded candy corn; there was always something I could find when I got tired of one of them.

You should think of investing in a similar manner. There's plenty of treats out there. Knock on a lot of different doors and find investments in various sectors and different industries. Having a mix of investments is part of having a diversified portfolio.

Diversification: *The process of mixing a variety of investments in an attempt to mitigate risk.*

Cold-Blooded

We've discussed a number of different ways to invest in this chapter. Now let's take a look at the investing mentality. What does it take to be a good investor? Anyone with money can lay down a position on a stock or a bond, but how do you know if you're doing the right thing? It starts by checking your emotions at the door.

Far too many people have gotten emotionally involved in their investments. So much so, in fact, that they forgot the initial reason as to why they got into the investment in the first place. Let's revisit our resident case study, Grace, to see how she handled one of her investments.

Grace has been solidly investing in her 401(k) for some time now and has recently opened up a brokerage account. The first investment Grace made was in the stock of ABC Company. She purchased the stock at $15.45 and the stock has gone up to $17.76.

Grace is feeling pretty confident about her decision and the company. A week later, ABC Company comes out with their annual earnings. They report that business has slowed from the previous year, and they lower their estimates for their earnings for next year. The stock takes a slide lower and opens up for trading the next day at $13.19.

Grace is now down on her investment nearly 15% from her original share purchase of $15.45. She decides to purchase more stock at this lower price to try and get back the money she lost. Grace pulls out some money from her 401k to buy more shares of ABC at this lower price in an attempt to 'make up' for the losses she has recently seen.

Did Grace do the right thing? Well, the company said they were expecting lower sales in the coming year than they had previously expected. The market heard that message and subsequently brought the stock price down to reflect that. Grace didn't get that message. She let her emotions dictate her decision to buy more stock of a company with decreasing earnings.

At the beginning of this book, I mentioned that money doesn't care. It has no feelings. The stock market is the same. It doesn't care what price you paid for something. You have to constantly re-assess your reasons for investing. And if the reasons you invested in something change, you should consider changing as well.

It's time to get excited about your money. Get involved with your investments and stay on top of your financial goals. Keep reading books on investing and broaden your knowledge of the many different ways there are to profit in the financial markets. You never know when that chip you lay down could turn into a life-changing opportunity for you.

9.
Developing

"When defeat comes, accept it as a signal that your plans are not sound, rebuild those plans, and set sail once more toward your coveted goal."

—*Napoleon Hill*

We are constantly evolving as we move through life. Our goals change as we change. We will go through peaks and valleys both in our finances and in our daily lives. Your goal should be to continue to develop and improve from where you are right now.

Personal growth and development will naturally occur through time. You will make mistakes. Learn from them. If you get knocked down 100 times in life, your ability to get back up 101 times is all that matters. Human motivation plays such a large role in money.

You will find that once you start paying attention to your money, your interest in maintaining that focus will increase as you start to have success. If you set a goal for yourself to have $5000 saved by the end of the year, and you attain that goal, watch out. Your success just became its own motivating factor.

Success

It is important to have success in your personal finances early on. A small win is still a win. When I was in debt collections, the hardest part of convincing someone to get back on track with their finances was getting them to make that first payment. Once I got them to do that, it was easy.

By relaying that small success to them in a positive manner, they understood that their actions had a positive consequence. They were able to see how it affected them on a direct, personal level. Success is like a drug. Once you get a taste, you just want more.

That success can start to build too. The faster an object is moving, the harder it is to stop. So how do you get moving in the right direction fast enough so you can't be stopped by a few bumps in the road? Motivation. You need to continue to motivate yourself on a daily basis so eventually, your actions become ingrained within you and they form a habit. In personal finance, that means thinking of the 'future you.'

The Future You

We all know that we need to save for retirement. So why is it so hard? We talked earlier about habits, and the need to form good habits when you are young. I think it all begins with that. If you can get started early, you will be both ahead of your peers and be able to capitalize on the benefits of compound interest. The more money you can save early in your life, the better off the 'future you' will be later in life.

We tend to forget about our future selves. The want and desire of the present can get so intense that it almost blinds us from the things yet to come. That will be a continuous struggle you will need to face. However, being disciplined to follow the plans that you lay out for yourself will counteract those desires.

For you visual learners out there, I have come up with a plan you can use in your financial journey to move forward in your personal development process. To introduce this, let's consider an example in the field of psychology to compare our financial lives to a theory that illustrates human motivation.

Maslow's Hierarchy of Needs

Psychologist Abraham Maslow developed a theory based on a hierarchy of needs in his paper "A Theory of Human Motivation" released in 1943. While I would recommend you read his paper, the purpose of highlighting Maslow's theory is the correlation it has to money and finances. In essence, this hierarchy assumes that people tend to fulfill their basic needs before they are motivated to fulfill the more complex needs that exist higher on the chart.

Consider the process of building a house. Your natural starting point would be the foundation. A solid support structure has to be in place before you can move on to anything else. The same is true of Maslow's theory. See the image below to view the various stages.

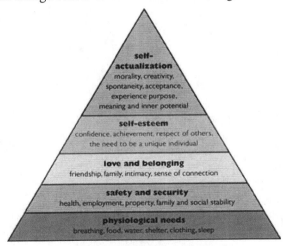

Maslow's Hierarchy of Needs

The Financial Parallel

The hierarchy of needs is a phenomenal glimpse into human motivation. Building on that idea of a foundation of needs, I have drawn a financial parallel to use as a guide when deciding where to place your money as you go through life. You can use these stages as a guide to ascend the financial hierarchy in the same way you would move up Maslow's Hierarchy of Needs. After you have your basic needs covered, you can start to think about the future.

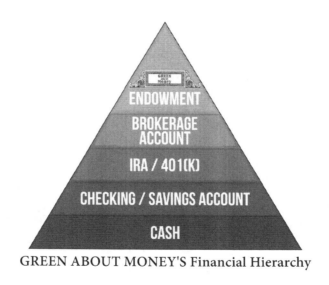

GREEN ABOUT MONEY'S Financial Hierarchy

Cash

The foundation of our financial pursuits. We all have to start somewhere. The money in your pocket is the rawest form of personal finance there is. You need this basic form of currency before you can proceed with anything else. And, if we're being honest, it makes good financial sense to always have a portion of your money in cash.

Checking/Savings Account

This is the safety stage. There are not a lot of risks here, and your money is easily accessible. You can accomplish most of your daily needs at this stage. There is an added level of safety as your money is protected under the umbrella of the bank's security. Revisit the section on banks before you make your decision on what type of account to open up.

IRA/401k

In the belonging stage, we are a part of something larger. If you are working for a company, you may have access to a 401k. If not, anyone with earned income can open an IRA. Both of these vehicles have unique contribution limits available to all Americans. The important concept here is that you can contribute to these accounts on a pre-tax basis. This lowers your taxable rate of income, allowing you to invest in yourself.

Brokerage Account

In this stage, you are confident in your financial position. Choose investments for yourself based on your research of the company and the industry in general. Understand that if investing in the stock market, your money will ebb and flow with current economic conditions. The key here is perseverance and diversification.

Endowment

Finally, we reach the self-actualization stage. This is the stage everyone seeks to reach. In this stage, we have a purpose and meaning. This is where we can use our money to do some good and give back. For many of us, that will mean passing something on to our children. One way to do that is to set up an educational fund for your children to access when they head off to college. A 529 Plan is an example of that.

529 Plan: A tax-advantaged plan that allows individuals to save and pay for future education costs, named after the numbered section of the IRS code in which it refers to (529).

Those who aren't planning on having children might consider looking outside the family to give back.

Giving

"We make a living by what we get, but we make a life by what we give."
—*Winston Churchill*

America is considered to be one of the most generous countries in the world. American charitable donations continue to reach record levels in the hundreds of billions of dollars today. Despite our perception by some people around the world, the United States shares, helps and gives when there is a need.

I am not just speaking about the government when describing America's generosity. We the people are generally a caring society. We live in a free nation, and are not forced to do anything with our money except pay our taxes and maintain our own financial responsibilities. Yet, foundations such as the American Red Cross get funded through our citizens on a continuous basis.

The point I am trying to make here is not to shame you into giving. It is to show you that you can do more when your own personal needs are met. American entrepreneurs such as J.D. Rockefeller, Henry Ford, and Bill Gates found that to be true, as did many others. Giving of your own free will can be one of the most satisfying things you can do in life. Are you a giving person?

Self-Worth

Do you believe you can succeed financially? That is one of the most important questions you can ask yourself. It is very hard to do something that your mind thinks is impossible. You have to believe in your ability to succeed. This book is not full of delusional ideas about how to get rich. These are sound financial principles. If you don't believe in yourself, you need to find out where that belief is coming from.

You need to ask yourself why you don't have faith in yourself. Many times this comes from our parents, friends, or even teachers who tell us that we are destined to walk down a certain path in life. If that is the case for you, stop listening and ask yourself what qualifies them to tell you how your life will turn out?

If you believe the pessimism that can get passed down from generation to generation, you will almost certainly give in to that way of thinking and fulfill that prophecy. You need to break that cycle. Don't let anyone tell you how much you are worth. Understand that this is all about you ~ nobody else.

We all develop in different ways. Most of you will have life events that knock you down the hierarchy of needs pyramid. Use that as a learning process and start climbing right back up. The 'future you' deserves that. And when you reach your goals, help out those who may not climb as fast as you. It starts with believing in your ability to succeed and recognizing your self-worth.

Conclusion

You have the tools to succeed now. Will you use them? I hope you have come up with a plan for yourself. If not, take time to do so now. As you know, those who fail to plan, plan to fail.

Most Americans are not abiding by the principles in this book. The consumer lifestyle is setting them up for failure. You have a chance to change that for yourself. Don't start your adult life saddled with debt. Instead, use your money to create a sustainable future for yourself. Set attainable goals, create good financial habits, and use the information in this book to build life-changing wealth for the 'future you.'

Thank you for the opportunity to allow me to share this information with you.

I hope you found tremendous value within these pages. If you've enjoyed this book, or simply recognize its worth, I would greatly appreciate if you could either recommend it to someone or review it on Amazon.

I'd like to leave you with one final quote.

When I was young I used to think that money was the most important thing in life; now that I am old, I know it is."

—*Oscar Wilde*

www.greenaboutmoney.com

Glossary

401(k) Plan: *A retirement savings plan established by companies that allows employees to contribute earned income through salary-reduction on a pre-tax basis.*

529 Plan: *A tax-advantaged plan that allows individuals to save and pay for future education costs, named after the numbered section of the IRS code in which it refers to (529).*

Accumulation Phase: *A period of time when the value of an annuity is being built up by the investor.*

Annuitization Phase: *A period of time when the annuitant receives payments from the annuity.*

Annuity: *A type of investment that builds up incremental cash value and then pays out those funds, plus any earned interest, to the annuitant or individual account holder.*

Asset: *Something an individual or company owns.*

Bond: *A debt instrument in which an entity pays interest to the certificate holder (investor) at a predetermined rate of interest and length of time.*

Brokerage Account: *A type of investment account that is set up between a licensed brokerage firm and investor, typically for the purchase of stocks or exchange-traded funds (ETF's).*

Capital Appreciation: An increase in the price of an asset.

Credit Union: A non-profit financial organization operated under a member-owned structure.

Chargeback: The return of funds to an account from the merchant, typically after a dispute on a transaction.

Compound Interest: Interest that is calculated on both the initial principal and any accrued interest.

Consumer Price Index (CPI): An index that measures the change in price of a basket of goods and services.

Direct Deposit: An arrangement in which electronic funds, such as salaries, are deposited directly into a recipient's account.

Discount Broker: A type of stockbroker who charges a lower fee for investment orders than a typical full-service broker.

Discount Rate: The interest rate charged by the Federal Reserve Bank when lending to commercial or other member banks.

Diversification: The process of mixing a variety of investments in an attempt to mitigate risk.

Earnings: The profit of a company displayed as after-tax net income.

Federal Insurance Contributions Act (FICA): A U.S. governmental law requiring the withholding of earned income, typically from a paycheck, to subsidize the funding of programs such as Social Security and Medicare.

Federal Reserve Bank: *The central bank of the United States whose duties include commercial lending and the control of money.*

Gross Income: *Total income, before deductions such as taxes and insurance.*

Health Savings Account (HSA): *A tax-advantaged savings account for medical purposes that is set up for individuals covered by high-deductible health plans.*

Individual Retirement Account: *A type of tax-advantaged investment account that allows individuals to save for retirement on a tax-deferred basis.*

Inflation: *The rise in the general level of prices resulting in the fall in value of a currency.*

Initial Public Offering (IPO): *The first stock offering of a company to the public.*

Interest: *The money paid by the borrower to the lender as a result of a loan of other financial obligation.*

Liability: *Something that is owed or that someone is responsible for.*

Medicare: *A U.S. federal health program set up for the benefit of the citizens.*

Money: *A medium of exchange that is circulated by a government or official organization usually consisting of paper bills and coins.*

Mutual Fund: An investment product that pools the funds of investors and invests them in stocks, bonds, and other types of assets.

Net Income: The income that remains after deductions such as taxes and insurance.

Net Worth: The financial result of subtracting an individual's liabilities from his or her assets.

Opportunity Cost: The money or benefit an individual could have received, but lost, due to following another course of action.

Overdraft: An account deficit resulting from processing a transaction for more money than an account holds.

Payday Loan: A short-term loan that is lent at a high rate of interest to be paid back with funds from subsequent paychecks.

Portfolio: A group of financial holdings that include cash, stocks and other securities.

Price-Earnings (P/E) Ratio: A ratio that values a company based on the company's share price in relation to their earnings per share.

Real Interest Rate: The rate an investor expects to receive after factoring the effects of inflation.

Rollover: The transfer of financial assets from one retirement plan to another without tax penalties.

ROTH IRA: *An individual retirement account that allows investors to use after-tax money to save for retirement and benefit tax-free withdrawals after a predetermined age.*

Security: *A financial instrument such as stocks or bonds that can be traded in the market.*

Shares: *An equal ownership unit of a company.*

Social Security: *A U.S. federal social program designed to give financial assistance to its citizens.*

Stock: *A financial security that signifies an ownership relationship to a company.*

Teaser Rate: *A low, introductory rate of interest offered for a fixed period of time in an attempt to gain new clients.*

Withholding: *The portion of earned income that is held back, or deducted, for purposes such as taxes and insurance.*

Withholding Allowance: *Exemptions made by employees on their tax forms to determine appropriate deduction amounts from their earned income.*

Further Study

These are some of my favorite things to read & study when it comes to gaining knowledge in the area of finance and investing.

Investopedia

This website is a wealth of information. If I couldn't afford to go to college and I was starting over, I would consider this my second Bible and just start learning. From financial definitions to articles to real-time market information, you really can't afford not to bookmark www.investopedia.com.

Books

- *The Intelligent Investor by Benjamin Graham*
- *Think And Grow Rich by Napolean Hill*
- *Jim Cramer's Get Rich Carefully by James J. Cramer*
- *The Total Money Makeover by Dave Ramsey*
- *Rich Dad, Poor Dad by Robert Kiyosaki*
- *The Richest Man In Babylon by George S. Clason*

Financial News

- CNBC
- FOX Business
- Cheddar

APPENDIX A:
FINANCIAL GOALS

Short-Term

_____
_____
_____
_____
_____
_____

Mid-Term

_____
_____
_____
_____
_____
_____

Long-Term

_____
_____
_____
_____
_____
_____

Appendix B:
Statement of Net Worth

Assets

Bank Accounts/Cash	$
Real Estate	$
Automobiles	$
Furnishings	$
Electronics	$
Jewelry	$
Stocks/Bonds/Mutual Funds	$
Business Interests	$
Other	$

Total Assets: _____

Liabilities

Mortgage(s)	$
Car Loan(s)	$
School Loan(s)	$
Personal Loans	$

Credit Cards	$ _____
Other Debt	$ _____

Total Liabilities: _____

Total Assets - Total Liabilities = Net Worth*: _____

*Net Worth Can Be a Positive or Negative Number

Appendix C:
5 Steps to Eliminate Debt

START BY LAYING EVERYTHING OUT IN FRONT OF YOU

1. Separate the balances that are less than $1000.
2. Of those, IMMEDIATELY ATTACK THE DEBT WITH THE LOWEST AMOUNT. Use any money you have available to do this. Focus everything on this one debt until you have paid it off. You will pay the MINIMUM AMOUNT DUE on the remainder of your debts.
3. Once you have finished the first one, move on to the NEXT LOWEST one until you have paid off all of you debts under $1000. You will continue to pay the minimum monthly payments on the remainder of your debts.
4. Next, FOCUS ON INTEREST RATES. Line up the remainder of your debts from highest to lowest in terms of the interest rates that you pay on them.
5. IMMEDIATELY ATTACK THE DEBT WITH THE HIGHEST INTEREST RATE and continue to pay the minimum monthly payments on the remainder of your debts.

CONTINUE DOWN THE LINE UNTIL YOU HAVE PAID OFF ALL OF YOUR DEBTS

The process is simple.
The question is: Are you able to do it?

Type of Debt	Interest Rate	Amount of Debt

Appendix D:
Monthly Budget

Income

Wages / Salaries (After Taxes)		$_____
Other Income	(+)	$_____
Total Income*	(=)	$_____

Expenses

	Recommended (%)	Actual ($)
Housing	25%	$_____
Transportation	12%	$_____
Savings/Investments	15%	$_____
Food	12%	$_____
Debt	9%	$_____
Utilities	8%	$_____
Insurance/Medical	7%	$_____
Personal	7%	$_____
Entertainment	5%	$_____
Total Expenses*		$_____

*Total Income and Total Expenses Should Be Equal

About the Author

Jeff Tarman is an American Entrepreneur, Investor and Author. He has been a student of finance since a young age. He has a Bachelor of Science Degree in Finance and has been state licensed in Business Law, Debt Collections, Insurance, and Real Estate.

Jeff has worked and studied in many different facets of the financial industry throughout his career, including starting and operating multiple small business ventures. An entrepreneur at heart, he has learned through experience as well as the classroom.

Follow him at www.jefftarman.com
Follow this book at www.greenaboutmoney.com